3D printing without prior knowledge - 7 days to your first 3D print:

Realising ideas without technical know-how

2nd edition

content

1. Different types of 3D printing 3

    1.1 Cartesian 3D printers: 5

    1.2 Polar 3D printer... 6

    1.3 Delta 3D printer 6

2 Classic structure of a Cartesian 3D printer 8

    2.1 The framework... 9

    2.2: The electronics... 11

    2.3 The mainboard.. 12

    2.4 The motors... 15

    2.5 Stepper motor driver 17

    2.6 The heating head 20

    2.7 Extruder motor.. 23

3. Comparison of filament types... 29

    3.1 PLA (polylactic acid) 29

    3.2 ABS (acrylonitrile butadiene styrene) 31

    3.3 ASA (acrylonitrile styrene acrylate)................................... 32

    3.4 PETG (polyethylene terephthalate glycol-modified) 33

    3.5 TPU (thermoplastic urethane) 34

    3.6 Nylon/Polyamide... 35

4 Which printer is right for me?.. 38

    4.1 Size and installation space 38

    4.2 Frame 40

    4.3 Electronics... 40

1. **Different types** of 3D printing

4.4 Miscellaneous...40

4.5 An overview of the current market 41

4.6 Which filament is for the printer? 46

5. First prints...48

5.1 From idea to machine code 48

5.2 From machine code to 3D printing..........................63

6. Maintenance and wear...70

6.1 Daily maintenance: 70

6.2 Weekly maintenance:..70

6.3 Monthly maintenance: 71

6.4 Maintenance every 3 - 6 months: 72

6.5 Further tips for long-lasting printing fun..............72

6.6 Spare parts...73

7. The most frequent causes of errors 76

7.1 No filament comes out of the nozzle 76

7.2 The object comes loose during printing 77

7.3 The corners of the print come loose - Warping ...78

7.4 Holes in print - (partial) under-extrusion 80

7.5 Too much material – over-extrusion.......................82

7.6 Printing has offset (layer shifting) 83

7.7 Thread formation (stringing) 84

7.8 You can see the filling lines on the outer walls....86

7.9. Bulging corners - elephant foot.............................87

7.10. The printing bed cannot be levelled....................88

8th bonus chapter – Gift idea: Lithophane pictures ...89

8.1 Lithophanes – what, how, why?................................89

8.2 Actual creation: 93

9 Summary and outlook 101

Free eBook in PDF format

Since the print of the book is done directly by Amazon and I have no control over the quality, details may be lost.

For this reason, I offer the eBook as a PDF file free of charge when you buy the book. In the PDF, all pictures are high-resolution and the version is the latest one.

More information at the end of the book.

Preface

Once a fascinating, budding technology, 3D printing has entered the mainstream in recent years. Whereas in the past thousands of euros had to be spent for a halfway decent 3D printer, 3D printers have now become affordable even for "average consumers" thanks to higher volumes and advancing technology.

In addition, you no longer need to be a mechanical or electrical engineer to understand how a 3D printer works. Many hobbyists are also interested in 3D printing, and for you, buying a printer is a good start but will not be enough.

Especially in the beginning, you will likely experience many setbacks and failed printing attempts before you reach the desired print quality. Without any previous knowledge, you must work your way through many forums or Facebook groups and help pages and gradually acquire all the essential skills in self-study – which can take years.

In order to help you get started quickly and not lose valuable time, we created this 3D printing "quick guide". It allows you to correct errors as quickly as possible and immerse yourself in the subject of 3D printing. By preparing yourself, you can avoid making the same mistakes as those before you.

With our guide, knowledge from personal experience along with technical background information are passed on to you in one compact package.

This book may serve as a guide for the first steps, so that you can get into the subject pf "3D printing" as quickly as possible without any previous knowledge. After reading this book, you will be able to print your first 3D models, understand all the settings and functions, and recognise and compensate for errors in 3D printing. The first step is to understand the general processes of a 3D printer.

1. Different types of 3D printing

3D printers have been around much longer than you might think. Back in 1981, Hideo Kodama in Japan published a report on an additive manufacturing process which is the forerunner to today's 3D printing concept.

There are many different types of 3D printers available today, and they can vary greatly in design, operation and performance. But for most, the basic idea is the same. The material to be worked on is gradually applied, combines with the existing material and "out of nowhere" (also called additive 3D printing) the model is created.

This contrasts with subtractive manufacturing processes, where material is taken away. For example, when an object is milled from a block of metal.

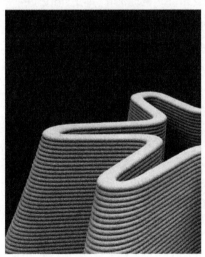

Nowadays, almost any material can be processed by 3D printers – whether plastics, resins, glass, metal, or even chocolate, or biomass such as organic tissue. Nearly anything can be used to make a three-dimensional print. The most common 3D materials are thermoplastics such as PLA, which is made from corn starch, or ABS, which is also used for sockets, toys (LEGO) or automotive parts. There are other materials used such as PETG, a modified form of PET known from plastic drink bottles, or flexible

Figure 1 Additive 3D printing of concrete

plastics such as thermoplastic polyurethanes (TPU), or even nylon, a well-known synthetic fibre.

Usually, granules of the material are melted down and processed into a roll

3

of filament, which is a thin thread with a diameter of 1.75 mm to 3 mm. More about the individual filament types with their advantages and disadvantages will be discussed in more detail in the chapter "Filament types".

Today, the most widespread form of processing these filaments by far is so-called Fused Deposition Modelling or Fused Layer Modelling (FDM/FLM). This is the most suitable method for the beginner. The material is heated above the melting point and laid out to cool in layers, so the 3D object is built from the bottom up, layer by layer.

FDM 3D printing is the most proven 3D printing method, both in industry and the private sector.

Other processes include stereolithography (SLA), which uses intense UV light to cause resins to cure, thereby creating an object, and laser sintering, in which metal or plastic powder is briefly melted and then cooled again.

SLA printers have also become more and more affordable for private individuals in recent years and are becoming increasingly popular – especially for very detailed applications such as model making. However, the material to be processed is usually a synthetic resin which reacts corrosively and should therefore only be used with face masks and gloves. For this reason, it is also not suitable for beginners.

Thus, we've dedicated this guide to the simplest and most widespread principle, FDM printing, i.e. the process of hot-melt printing. The 3D printers for this technique are the most affordable and most popular. If difficulties arise, there are hundreds of people who have already had the same problem, so there is probably a well-tested solution. Among the FDM printers, there are "Cartesian 3D printers", "polar 3D printers" and "delta 3D printers".

1. **Different types** of 3D printing

1.1 Cartesian 3D printers:

Cartesian 3D printers are by far the most widely used because they are very easy to manufacture, maintain and program. As a result, they have become widely accepted, which in turn has reduced manufacturing costs.

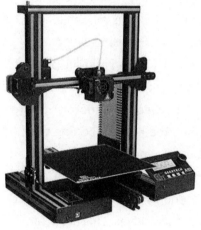

The Cartesian coordinate system is the familiar one. There are three directions of travel X, Y, Z (width, depth, height) which run independently of one another. One motor is responsible for each direction (or several motors connected in parallel if the load is too heavy for one motor). If you want to move one step to the left, one motor moves the print head to the left.

Figure 2 Cartesian 3D printer

1.2 Polar 3D printer

With a polar 3D printer, the polar co-ordinate system is the basis for the position description. X and Y are not used, but a radius and an angle. The height, however, is still called Z. The print rotates on a round printing plate. The advantage of the polar 3D printer is that it only needs two motors: one to determine the height and one that rotates the printing bed while, at the same time, moving it linearly in one

Figure 3 Polar 3D printer

direction. This makes polar 3D printers more energy efficient. However, polar 3D printers have not been able to establish themselves. This has to do with the increased computational effort and non-intuitive travels, as people think in three-dimensional coordinates. Also, the bed is more difficult to maintain.

1.3 Delta 3D printer

A delta printer has a fundamentally different structure, with all axes moving independent-ly of one another. So if you want to move one step to the left, all three axes must be moved. The illustration shows such a 3D printer. The main advantages of the delta printer compared to the Cartesian print set-up are higher accuracy and higher maximum

Figure 4 Delta 3D printer

1. Different types of 3D printing

printing speeds. They are also generally lighter and perfectly suited for narrow, tall objects. The disadvantage is that a much larger installation space is required than the dimensions of the object to be printed. If you want to print a 30 cm high object, the Cartesian printer only needs to be a few centimetres higher. A delta printer, on the other hand, tends to be twice as high.

Moreover, we are used to thinking along the "normal", Cartesian system in our everyday life, so the movements of the delta printer's axes are not always easy to follow. In addition to the three printer systems discussed, there are, among others, robot arm 3D printers and conveyor belt 3D printers.

Cartesian printers are most commonly found in both domestic and industrial use. These printers are perfect for beginners.

2 Classic structure of a Cartesian 3D printer

The first printers in the consumer sector were do-it-yourself kits, but these can no longer be recommended. You had to replace just about every part, be it the frame, motors or belts, to get a reliable and durable printer. You learnt and grew with the printer, but you would spend far more time troubleshooting than actually printing. Furthermore, these printers were not only unfriendly to beginners in many respects, such as security, electronics or stability, but were simply outdated.

Figure 5 Elegoo Neptune Front

In the meantime, many manufacturers have focused on the private 3D printing sector. Most of these companies are located in Asia.

We will first discuss the different components of a 3D printer. A beginner-friendly printer for illustration is the Elegoo Neptune 3D printer. It is an entry-level to mid-range printer. It is the perfect reference for explaining the functions of a 3D printer and the way to the first print.

2 Classic structure of a Cartesian 3D printer

2.1 The framework

A 3D printer first consists of a frame or a frame on which all other components are mounted.

Precision is the key to 3D printing. If the frame is not correctly aligned, the material is not able to withstand the stresses and strains, and screws that are a little loose can significantly negatively impact the print result.

That is why the frame is one of the most important components of the 3D printer. With cheap models, the frame is made of plastic, possibly acrylic, or wood. In higher quality models, it is made of more torsion-resistant materials such as aluminium or steel. Many 3D printers use

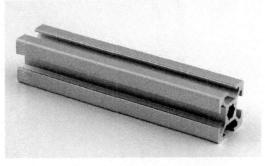

Figure 6 Standard 20x20mm aluminium profile

20x20mm or 30x30mm aluminium profiles. These standard sizes are inexpensive and well-tested.

In 3D printing, there are a lot of parts which move quickly, such as the printing bed or the X carriage. Each of these parts has a so-called moment of inertia, which depends on the mass and the speed of travel. The frame must be able to absorb these forces. Furthermore, high acceleration values cause vibrations at the printer. Many of these vibrations oscillate in the audible range, up to about 15 kHz, and certain frequencies of vibration can cause additional stress to the printer because of so-called resonance effects. Basically, every physical object is actually vibrating at a natural frequency based on its geometry. If the object is externally excited with vibrations at this frequency, it vibrates more strongly at the same frequency.

The best-known example, which at the same time shows what negative effects resonance effects can have, is the accident of the Tacoma Narrows Bridge, which was a suspension bridge in the USA. The Tacoma Narrows Bridge had a very unfavourable design; even light wind vortices could cause the bridge to resonate. The bridge would flutter as if it was made of rubber.

Figure 7 Tacoma Narrows Bridge collapse

What was initially a tourist attraction came to an end in 1940. When a storm came, the bridge was so energised that it kept on swinging until finally two supporting cables broke and the bridge collapsed. Although this accident did not cost human lives, this event illustrates the importance of avoiding resonance effects.

In relation to our 3D printer, this means that vibrations of any kind must be minimised. The simplest way to do this is to increase the weight and ensure that the individual components are firmly connected. As a result, the components become a larger body with increased mass and the resonance frequencies are reduced. Loose ball bearings can also cause audible resonance effects, which can be transmitted to the frame via the shafts or profiles.

A stiffer and more stable frame means lower chance of vibration or resonance. A more stable 3D printer yields better print results.

2.2: The electronics

The next component is the printer electronics. This is usually mounted in or on the frame. With some models, the electronics are also installed in an external unit. The electronics consist of several individual parts, for example the power supply (the power pack), the computing unit, i.e. the "brain" of the printer and the display. In the Elegoo Neptune 3D printer, the power supply unit and the computer unit are built into the frame for safety reasons and are therefore not visible or accessible. Many manufacturers are tending more and more to use a similar closed design for the electronics.

Often, 24V or 12V direct current is used as the operating voltage. For large printers that require a lot of heating power, the trend is towards a 230V AC power supply for the heating bed and 24V DC power supply for the logic electronics. Again and again, you hear about scorched contacts or short circuits in 3D printers. In most cases, however, it is not the electronics that are faulty, but unsuitable power connections with insufficient cable cross-sections or undersized connectors.

Most power supply units are harmless, but it is advisable to have preparatory protective measures, such as a smoke detector and fire extinguisher, at hand, especially if working with an inexpensive entry-level model.

Next is the heart of the electronics – the motherboard, or mainboard. All motors, sensors, the display and the power supply are connected to this board.

2.3 The mainboard

Figure 8 Mainboard with pluggable drivers and ATMega2560 chip

In order to make 3D printing available to a wide range of people, the RepRap project was launched in 2005. The aim was to develop an affordable 3D printer that anyone could build themselves, using simple means. Most domestic 3D printers are therefore based on this open source project. The firmware, comparable to the operating system of a PC, is called Marlin and is also "open source" and accessible to everyone. Even well-known 3D manufacturers like Creality or Geeetech use a modified form of Marlin as the firmware for their 3D printers.

2 **Classic structure** of a Cartesian 3D printer

Figure 9 ATMEGA2560 microprocessor

An ATmega2560 chip is often used as the computing unit, which is permanently installed on the mainboard. The chip is a proven microprocessor. It processes commands, controls the motors and thus brings the whole printer to life. The ATmega2560 chip quickly gained popularity, because the chip was already known among hobbyists and was very popular for other projects.

Perhaps some readers are familiar with Arduino. This is a programmable microprocessor series that has become very popular among hobby programmers. The largest microcontroller in the Arduino range, the Arduino MEGA, uses the ATmega2560 chip as standard. The advantage of this chip is that it can be easily programmed by the consumer using the Arduino IDE software, allowing changes or modifications to be made to the printer. These can then be adapted in the firmware. For example, if you replace the temperature sensor, you can enter the new sensor in the software so that the revised version is installed on the printer.

However, many manufacturers of complete systems do not release their source code, which makes it impossible for the end user to modify anything on the printer.

Despite its advantages, the ATmega2560 chip occasionally reaches its limits in terms of computing speed. The reason for this is the internal architecture of the processor. Like many other 3D printer chips, the chip is based on an

13

8-bit architecture, which has its drawbacks.

Because of the technological limitations for computing operations, other approaches and alternatives are being looked for in the development of 3D printers.

Microprocessors with internal 32-bit architecture, such as the STM32F chip, are an alternative. This offers additional advantages such as more internal memory or a clock frequency that is up to six times higher. This is why companies such as MKS, which specialises in mainboards for 3D printers, use this chip on many of their newer mainboards.

For example, this chip is located on the mainboard "MKS Robin (Mini)", which is built into many newer 3D printers as well as the Elegoo Neptune. As a result of the increased computing power, for example, printing the same exact figure on the Elegoo Neptune takes 10.45 hours while it takes 11.54 hours on a comparable printer with an 8-bit system.

Microprocessors based on a 32-bit architecture are more powerful and have shorter printing times compared to 8-bit versions.

Depending on the type of printer, the electronic equipment may include other special features such as a touch display, a WLAN interface or a sensor that sounds an alarm when the filament runs out. The electronics also include the motors and their control, which are discussed in the following chapter.

2 Classic structure of a Cartesian 3D printer

2.4 The motors

Figure 10 Nema17 stepper motor

Since the motors have to work very precisely, stepper motors are used for this purpose. Stepper motors are synchronous motors. Inside them are many individual magnets and pairs of coils. Figure 10 shows the construction of the stator, which is equipped with coils. The rotatably mounted shaft forms the rotor. This is equipped with permanent magnets.

Each time the motors are activated, the motor shaft moves a fraction of a revolution – one step. The size of a step depends on the number of pole pairs.

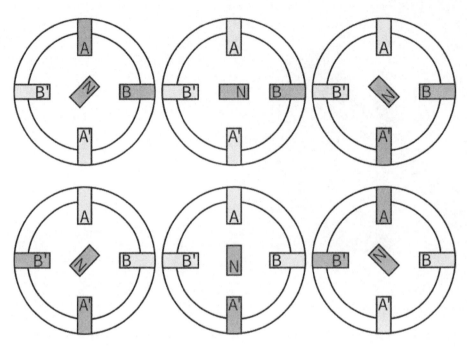

Figure 11 Schematic structure of a stepper motor

Figure 11 illustrates how the stepper motor works. The coils of the stator are reversed once per step so that the permanent magnet rotates to a fixed position. With two pairs of coils, eight possible states are thus created.

The most common stepper motors are NEMA17 stepper motors or, for larger printers, NEMA34 motors. The bipolar versions of these motors require, for example, 200 steps for one full revolution. This means that the motor rotates 1.8° per step (360° divided by 200 steps).

2.5 Stepper motor driver

The stepper motor still needs a component for control, that is, a stepper motor driver (stepper driver). The stepper driver receives information from the ATmega2560 chip, for example, about how many steps the motor should rotate and controls the motor accordingly. The stepper motor drivers (one for each motor) are either exchangeably plugged into the mainboard or integrated into the electronic board of the printer and cannot be exchanged or retrofitted.

In addition to the noise from moving parts and the fan, the drivers also have a decisive influence on the noisiness of the printer.

The reason for this is the modulation of the control signals. To ensure perfect rotation of the motors, the motor must be controlled with a pure sine wave.

A perfect sine wave consists of a single oscillation without harmonic distortion. However, cheap stepper motor drivers cannot produce a completely clean sine wave, and this leads to various audible effects. There could be noticeable sound impulses, buzzing, hissing and beeping. A4988 motor drivers, for example, are cheap – less than one euro – but very loud and noisy.

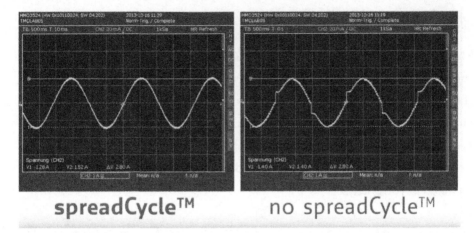

spreadCycle™   no spreadCycle™

Figure 12 Comparison of stepper motor control

Motor drivers from Trinamic, for example, are much more pleasant. The German company, which is active in the field of "motion control", has developed patented control methods that make motor movements quieter. These include the TMC2208 or TMC213 motor drivers.

They are whisper-quiet and have other advantages such as better, more powerful control of the motors and smoother resulting movements. The cost is about €10 per driver. Figure 12 shows the harmonic sine control (spreadCycle) in comparison with a control without spreadCycle technology.

Figure 13 TMC2208 chip

If you plan to use a 3D printer in an inhabited room, quieter motor drivers (in addition to quieter fans) are essential for acceptable noise levels.

Step losses:

The rotor of the stepper motor always follows the externally applied magnetic field. If external load torque prevents this, steps are "skipped". Skipping can happen, among other reasons, because the friction of the driven components is too high or the acceleration is too high. For a 3D printer, this means that the information about the current position of the shaft is lost. An offset is formed on the print object and the printing must be stopped. Therefore, step losses should be avoided at all costs. This can be achieved by reducing the external load torque or by applying a higher voltage to the motors. All stepper motor drivers, including the A4988 and TMC2208, have an adjustable reference voltage. If step losses occur, the voltage can be increased and more power can be assigned to the motor.

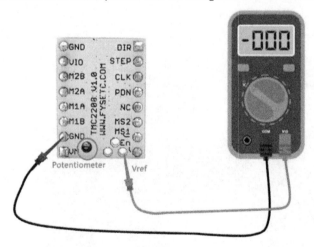

Figure 14 Setting the FYSETC TMC2208 driver

However, this results in higher power consumption and higher heat generation of the motors and drivers. The drivers must therefore be actively cooled. The maximum permissible reference voltage of the drivers depends on the maximum motor current and heating and can be found on the data sheet. For A4988 drivers, the reference voltage is 0.8-1.2V, and for TMC2208 drivers, it is 0.5-0.8V.

However, you should always try to minimise frictional losses before increasing the voltage. This protects the motors, the drivers and the moving parts.

To convert the rotation of the motor into a linear forward movement, a toothed belt (or threaded rods for high-precision printers) is used. It is important that the belt is taut, otherwise it will not be guided precisely. Cheaper models are made of rigid rubber, while higher quality belts such as a GT2 belt are interspersed with glass fibres and are more flexible. More flexible belts usually cost only a few euros and can improve the printed image.

2.6 The heating head

Figure 15 Print head with (left) and without (right) cover

The heart of the 3D printer is the movable print head, which is mounted on

2 Classic structure of a Cartesian 3D printer

a carriage to which the toothed belt is attached. It consists of
- a nozzle, which focuses the emerging filament and thus determines the width of the emerging material,

- a heating element, which is inserted into a heating block,

- a temperature sensor and

- a heat sink.

The nozzle is screwed directly into the heating block. The heating block is screwed into the heat sink by means of a threaded tube (called heatbreak or throat). The nozzle, heating block and heat sink form the so-called hotend.

During printing, the material should only be processed in the "liquid" and "solid" states. To avoid intermediate states, the heat sink is usually actively cooled with a fan (see Figure 15). Printers with a large heating block, mostly in industry, also have an additional water cooling system. The heating cartridge can optionally be fitted with a silicone cover to reduce heat dissipation. The graphic (Figure 16) illustrates the structure of the hotend. Furthermore, there is a component fan for cooling the extruded filament, which blows just under the nozzle and allows the filament and the already printed area to cool down as quickly as possible so that the print cannot run. Without this cooling, the still semi-liquid material runs uncontrolled.

THE HOTEND

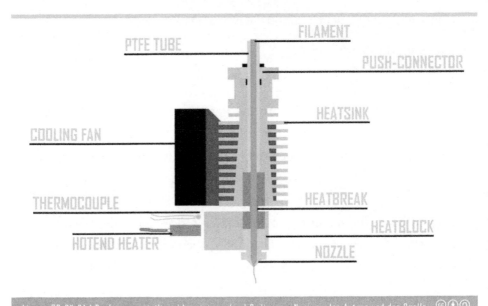

Figure 16 The structure of a 3D printer hotend - Infographic by Sercan Kahraman, CC-BY-SA; source: threedom.de

Different nozzle sizes:

Various nozzles are offered on the market with different sized openings. The openings range from 0.15mm to 1.2mm or even larger. On all standard consumer 3D printers, the nozzle has an M6 thread and a nozzle opening of 0.4mm. Since the nozzle diameter indicates the minimum width of the extrusion, a different nozzle opening can be used if needed. For example, a 0.2mm nozzle can be used for a very detailed print. The advantage here is the higher print accuracy. The disadvantage is that the nozzle can clog more easily and the print takes longer. The maximum printable layer height is also

22

smaller. As a rule of thumb, the maximum layer height is approximately 80% of the nozzle opening, so a 0.4mm nozzle would have a maximum layer height of 0.32mm and a 0.2mm a maximum layer height of 0.16mm.

On the other hand, you can also use a nozzle with a larger opening diameter, for example a 0.8 nozzle. However, it should be noted that doubling the diameter means a quadrupling of the opened area and thus also a quadrupling of the filament flow, i.e. how much filament has to be melted per time unit by the heater cartridge. If printing speeds are too high, the heating cartridge may reach its limit and no longer heat the high quantities of filament homogeneously. The outgoing filament then becomes more viscous in the core than in the outer areas and the pressure becomes uneven. In addition, the material needs more time to solidify again after leaving the nozzle. This can also be remedied by reducing the printing speed. A nozzle opening of 0.3-0.5mm is considered a good compromise. A 0.15 or 0.8 nozzle makes sense in special cases, but then you have to be prepared for additional challenges.

2.7 Extruder motor

The motor that pushes the filament through the print head, that is, through the heat sink, throat, heating block and nozzle, is called an extruder motor, or simply an extruder. The extruder is one of the most important components, as it ensures even supply of the filament. Nema17 motors are also used as extruder motors. The filament is fed by means of a gear wheel and pressed

Figure 17 Extruder motor with BMG attachment

into the hotend.

There are various types of extruders (BMG extruders, MK8 extruders, etc.), which may use gears to generate a higher torque.

If the extruder is mounted directly on the print head and travels on the carriage, this is known as a direct-drive design. This is useful for flexible filaments, for example, where the distance between the extruder motor and the heating block should be kept as short as possible. The disadvantage of this design is that the additional weight of the motor rides along with it all the time, and if you remember the inertia from physics lessons, you will quickly realise that it takes a lot of force to accelerate and decelerate the carriage including the extruder motor with every movement. A *Bowden* setup is a solution for this. Here, the extruder is detached from the carriage and attached to the printer frame.

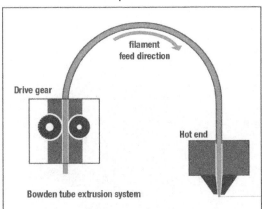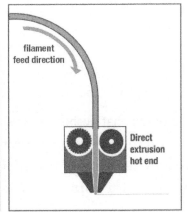

Figure 18 Bowden (right) and direct-drive (left) extruder

The filament is fed from the extruder into the heating block by means of a PTFE tube. This means that most of the weight from the direct-drive setup is removed and higher accuracy can be achieved at the same speed. In addi-

tion, the motors do not have to work as hard. On the other hand, the filament now rubs against the inside of the PTFE tube, which the extruder motor has to compensate with more force. With large printers and high speed,
and thus when a lot of filament has to be pushed through the heating block
quickly, the extruder might not have enough force to push the filament
through the hose and into the heating block. In this case, the already mentioned gear on the extruder motor must be used to increase the force.

With entry-level printers, the pressure chamber and thus the length of the
Bowden hose and the speed are too low for this effect to occur. Therefore,
a Bowden setup is usually no problem and is standard on most printers today. Direct-drive is almost only used for flexible filaments.

To enable the print head and the moving heating bed to move, the carriage
is usually fitted with ball, roller or slide bearings, which can move with relatively little friction on guide rails or linear guides.

When less friction is generated during the movements, less load is placed on
the motors and bearings which have to overcome this frictional force and
the printed image is cleaner.

Therefore, maintenance of the moving elements is essential. The maintenance of the various parts is dealt with in more detail in the chapter
"Maintenance and wear". In common Cartesian 3D printer models, the print
head moves in the X and Z (left and right; up and down) or X and Y (left and
right; back and forth) axes.

Now that you understand the movement of the print head, we will look at
the surface on which the object is printed – the print bed.

As just mentioned, the model is built up from bottom to top (in the Z-
direction), layer by layer. It is therefore important that the printing bed, that
is, the plate on which the object is printed, is very flat. In addition, the fila-

ment must adhere well to the printing bed at the beginning of the print so the object does not detach from the printing bed during printing. Therefore, many printing beds have a slightly roughened surface, kind of like sandpaper, or a special coating so that the filament can adhere to the tiny "mountains and valleys" (in the micrometre range).

There are manufacturers who specialise specifically in highly adhesive printing bed films – so you can see how important this aspect is. Since the adhesion of the most common filaments, such as PLA, ABS or PETG, is also greatly increased by warm substrates, most printing beds are heated. The print bed may then be referred to as a heated bed. Before each print, the printing bed is heated up to about 50°C (for PLA) to over 100°C (for ABS). Too little heat on the printing bed can often be the cause of various problems, which will be explained later in this chapter.

Sometimes the printer is also housed in an airtight compartment, which itself is heated. Why this is necessary for processing various materials such as ABS or nylon is explained in more detail in the chapter on filament types.

Such an enclosure, however, is reserved for printers in the upper price range. Therefore, the focus is on printers with a heatable bed, but without a (heated) housing. Furthermore, one should make sure that the print bed is parallel to the print head, as the layer thicknesses are in the hundredth micrometre range. This problem is usually solved with springs or silicone dampers, which are placed in the corners of the heating bed and can be precisely adjusted in height by a screw mechanism. The parallel alignment of the heating bed to the print head is also called "leveling".

The next question is:

How does the printer actually know where it's pointing?

The answer is relatively simple. First, the printer moves all axes back to the stop. End-stop switches are fitted there. These are normal switches that are triggered by touch. There are manual pressure switches or contactless end-stops, for example light barrier switches. If the print head hits an end-stop switch for the X direction, the motors are stopped by the software and the printer knows at that moment that it has arrived at the zero position in the X direction. From there, the stepper motors can move the printer back to the right, so, in the positive X-direction. The printer remembers the number of steps taken. The number of steps corresponds to the distance from the zero position. This system is used for all axes. If the printer moves all axes back to "zero", it is said that the print head is in the home position at X=0, Y=0 and Z=0 (abbreviated (0,0,0)).

If something does not go as planned during printing, for example an axle jams and cannot move, the printer does not "know" this. The printer "thinks" accordingly that it has moved on and assumes that it is now in a different position than it actually is. The print fails.

A single faulty movement therefore affects all subsequent movements. After the printer has initially moved to (0,0,0) (it is said to have been "homed"), the motors start moving the print head to the heating bed to print the first layer.

Autolevelling:

In addition to the already mentioned manual levelling by adjusting screws, there is also the possibility of auto-levelling. This uses a sensor located on the print head and at a fixed distance from the print nozzle. It measures the height of various points on the heating bed and passes this information on to the computing unit, which compensates for the height differences in the software. If the print head moves to a corner that is further down than the others (even if only micrometres), the motors move down in the Z-direction and compensate for these lower spots.

In most cases, non-contact sensors such as capacitive sensors or inductive sensors are used. These trigger from a certain proximity of the printing bed (often in the range of a few millimetres) and thus replace the Z limit switch. Although these sensors are useful, they only detect the symptoms and do not compensate or adjust the actual cause, namely the inclined printing bed.

3. Comparison of filament types

Before we introduce the 3D printers in the affordable price category, we will clarify which material, for our case which filament, is best suited for different applications. Model-making applications demand high attention to detail and less on weather resistance or food safety. 3D-Printed garden gnomes, on the other hand, should degrade in structure after the first frost. We present the most common filaments that can be processed with an affordable FDM 3D printer and compare the advantages and disadvantages.

3.1 PLA (polylactic acid)

PLA is by far the most widely used material in the hobby of 3D printing. And there are good reasons for this. PLA consists of many lactic acid molecules attached to each other and is therefore often called polylactic acid. Although PLA does not occur naturally, it is produced from natural, renewable sugar molecules, usually from corn starch, by means of a multi-stage synthesis. PLA can also be biodegraded under industrial composting conditions: 60-70°C, controlled humidity, etc.

> It is often suggested, particularly by PLA manufacturers, that PLA is environmentally sound and biodegradable under normal conditions. This is not true. PLA should be treated like any other plastic.

But why is PLA so popular in both non-commercial and industrial 3D printing? PLA has several advantages over ABS, PETG and many other filaments. First of all, it is very easy to use for printing. It has a low melting point of about 160°C and can be processed at about 180°C – 230°C. The melting point is the temperature at which the material changes from a *solid* to a (viscous) *liquid* state. Since the filament is processed in the *liquid* state, the processing temperature is correspondingly higher than the melting point. The shrinkage of PLA is also relatively low. This means that the material does not shrink as much as ABS, for example, when it cools down. Furthermore, with PLA, a heating bed is not necessary for adhesion. It is also very pleasant for the user to print with, as it does not release any toxic vapours into the ambient air during processing, so it can be printed without an enclosure or fume extraction. Because it is made from corn starch or another renewable resource, it is also one of the most environmentally friendly 3D printing filaments. The breaking strength of PLA is moderately high, but for load applications such as gears it is only conditionally suitable to unsuitable. Although PLA consists of lactic acid, it is not food safe due to processing residues.

Other substances can also be added to the PLA filament, such as metal, wood, fluorescent or electrically conductive particles. If a "wood filament" is found, it is most likely to be PLA mixed with wood particles. When processing this type of PLA hybrid filament, care must be taken to ensure that the proper print settings for the filament are used. Wood particles can clog the nozzle more easily, and metal particles (such as iron or bronze) wear out the printer's brass nozzle, which is cheap and widely used, due to abrasion.

For example, a 0.4mm nozzle is ready for the bin after one kilogram of PLA filament containing metal particles. This can be remedied with higher quality nozzles made of hardened steel. If only the appearance of metal is needed for the 3D object, a bronze-coloured PLA filament, for example, which contains only colour pigments and no real bronze particles, is recommended.

There are also many modified forms of PLA, such as PLA+, which has a higher impact resistance. However, the basic properties differ only slightly from

3. Comparison of filament types

standard PLA.

PLA is proven, easy to process and easy to modify. Thus PLA filaments are suitable for many applications and are especially suitable for newcomers.

Summary of PLA

Print difficulty: easy, very beginner-friendly

Print temperature: 180 - 230 °C

Printing bed temperature: 0 - 70° C (adhesion-related)

Weatherproof: no

Shelf life: medium to high

Shrinkage: hardly

Breaking strength: medium

Flexibility: low to medium

Food safe: normally no, see manufacturer's instructions

3.2 ABS (acrylonitrile butadiene styrene)

After PLA, ABS is the second most popular plastic for 3D printing. Like PLA, ABS is produced synthetically. Unlike ABS, it is not based on vegetable sugar components, but on substances from crude oil, more precisely the eponymous butadiene and styrene.

ABS has been used in industry for a long time, so it is tried and tested. Lego bricks, sockets and much more are produced with ABS. In the field of 3D printing, it is often used for engineering applications or for the production of prototypes. ABS is also used in the automotive industry, for example for auto body parts. As with virtually any type of filament material, particles can be added to ABS to slightly change its properties.

The main advantages of ABS are weather resistance, high stiffness, strength and toughness. For 3D printing with ABS filaments, a heating plate is indispensable, as the shrinkage of ABS is much higher than that of PLA.

A heated bed with a temperature of approx. 100-120 °C is recommended. To reach such temperatures, a heatable chamber for the printer is usually recommended. This also has the advantage that toxic vapours, which are produced during 3D printing of ABS, cannot enter the living area.

Another disadvantage of shrinkage is that the whole object contracts and its corners lift off the printing bed. In other words, there is warping of the object.

Summary of ABS
Printing difficulty: medium to high
Print temperature: 210 - 250 °C
Printing bed temperature: 90 - 130° C (adhesion-related)
Weatherproof: medium to high - but vulnerable to UV radiation
Durability: high
Shrinkage: strong
Breaking strength: medium to high
Flexibility: medium to high
Food safe: no

3.3 ASA (acrylonitrile styrene acrylate)

ASA is produced by copolymerisation of acrylonitrile and styrene and is also a popular material in industry. It is used, for example, for brackets, ventilation grilles and play equipment for indoor and outdoor use.

ASA has the advantages of ABS, primarily its stability and strength, but has the decisive advantage of not being susceptible to UV radiation. It is also easier to process.

ASA warps much less than ABS, so a lower heating bed temperature can be used. For these reasons, ASA is generally much easier to process than ABS and is somewhat comparable to PLA.

Summary of ASA
Print difficulty: easy to medium
Print temperature: 230 - 270 °C
Printing bed temperature: 60 - 120° C (adhesion-related)
Weatherproof: yes
Durability: high
Shrinkage: light to medium
Breaking strength: medium to high
Flexibility: medium to high
Food safe: no

3.4 PETG (polyethylene terephthalate glycol-modified)

PET is a familiar material in everyday life, especially in the form of PET bottles. PETG is virtually the same material, but glycol is added to the PET structure. The resulting plastic has a lower viscosity when melted and is suitable for 3D printing. The viscosity describes how easily a material flows. A high viscosity material which doesn't readily flow is not desirable for 3D printing. Similarly to PET, PETG is transparent and nearly crystal clear if no colourants are added.

PETG is used for food containers, vases and medical equipment. PETG is easy to process, nearly odourless and in many cases food safe. It is just as impact resistant as ABS or ASA, but not quite as resistant to breakage.

Summary of PETG

Print difficulty: easy to medium

Print temperature: 210 - 240 °C

Printing bed temperature: 50 - 80° C (adhesion-related)

Weatherproof: yes

Durability: high

Shrinkage: light

Breaking strength: medium to medium high

Flexibility: medium to high

Food safe: yes (observe manufacturer's instructions)

3.5 TPU (thermoplastic urethane)

Next, there are flexible TPU plastics. Unlike PLA or ABS, TPU does not refer to a specific material, but a series of materials, namely the thermoplastic urethanes. Accordingly, the various materials differ in their properties such as viscosity, elasticity or printability. However, the term TPU is still generally used as if it referred to as a single material. TPU is found, for example, in protective cases such as mobile phone covers. TPU is the most widely used elastoplastic material in the 3D printing business. The elasticity of TPU is specified with the so-called Shore hardness, like it is for silicones.

Since TPU belongs to the soft elastomers, the Shore A hardness scale is used. A 1kg calibration weight is pressed on a 6mm thick material sample for 15 seconds and the depth of penetration of the test weight into the material is measured. The Shore value of 0 corresponds to a penetration depth of 2.5mm and the Shore value 100A to a penetration depth of 0mm. Most TPU filaments use Shore hardnesses of 95A. Ninjaflex TPU filaments, which are extremely flexible, come to Shore hardnesses of 60A because of the added softeners. There are even more flexible filaments with Shore hard-

3. Comparison of filament types

ness of 40A.

The advantages of TPU are its many different applications, for example in seals, the aforementioned mobile phone covers or model car tyres.

During processing, please note that the extruder must press the flexible filament through the hot end (nozzle). Due to its softness, TPU is a very demanding material for extruders. The extruder gear wheel finds less adhesion with flexible filaments. Therefore, slow printing speeds (20 - 30mm/s) are recommended for TPU. Furthermore, a direct-drive extruder is clearly advantageous, because it avoids the additional friction that would occur within the Teflon tube.

Summary of TPU

Printing difficulty: medium

Print temperature: 200 - 240 °C

Printing bed temperature: 0 - 60° C (adhesion-related)

Weatherproof: low - medium

Durability: high

Shrinkage: light

Breaking strength: high to very high (flexible)

Flexibility: high (depending on Shore hardness)

Food safe: no (observe manufacturer's instructions)

3.6 Nylon/Polyamide

Lastly, nylon is a popular filament among hobby 3D printmakers. Nylon is a family of polyamides (PAs). PA6 (or nylon-6) and PA66 (or nylon-6,6) make up 95% of the market. Others such as PA12 play only a secondary role. Nylon is probably best known from cable ties, cords or drone propellers. Nylon is very flexible yet tear-resistant. It has low friction and is therefore used to 3D print, for example, gears that are designed for high speeds with low friction losses.

Similar to TPU filaments, nylon is much more demanding in processing, adheres less to the printing bed and must therefore be printed slowly.

Nylon can also be further reinforced with glass fibre, for example, which makes it a widely used material for special applications, especially in industry.

Summary of nylon
Printing difficulty: high
Print temperature: 235 - 260 °C
Printing bed temperature: 80 - 110° C (adhesion-related)
Weatherproof: medium to high
Durability: high
Shrinkage: medium
Breaking strength: very high (flexible)
Flexibility: high
Food safe: no (observe manufacturer's instructions)

Of course, there are many niche filaments that are intended for a very specific application. However, the five types of filaments that have been discussed cover approximately 99% of all possible FDM 3D printing applications.

3. Comparison of filament types

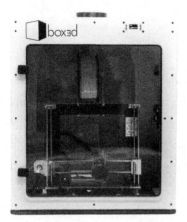

Figure 19 Example of a pressurised chamber

It should be noted that some filaments such as ABS or nylon react strongly to temperature fluctuations. An open window can have a negative effect on the print, as the ambient temperature and pressure change more quickly. In order to create constant ambient conditions, it is recommended to process these filaments in a closed pressure chamber. This should also be equipped with a fire alarm and a high-quality air filter. Among hobbyists, the construction of enclosures for the 3D printer has become a real sport.

4 Which printer is right for me?

The fact that the 3D printer market has grown exponentially in recent years is great. However, you are now spoilt for choice, as the number of different printers seems endless. If you enter the term "3D printer" into Amazon, more than 60,000 results appear there alone. But don't worry – we will go through all your needs and analyse them step by step. That way you will find the perfect printer for you.

4.1 Size and installation space

Not everyone has a dedicated hobby cellar or 2 x 2 m storage space available, so the dimensions of the printer are a basic but important aspect. There are both compact printers that measure only 30 x 30 x 50 cm and printers that can take up a cubic metre (one metre long, high and wide).

Therefore before buying, you should ask yourself the questions: What do I want to print, anyway? What is the size? Do I have space for a machine that prints this size object?

The maximum size object that you can print with a 3D printer depends on the printing volume, that is, the size of the print bed on which you are printing and the maximum height that the printer can print.

You should always use the smallest possible printing bed that still suits your needs, otherwise heating takes longer and power consumption is higher than necessary. If you only want to print figures up to 15 cm, a 30cmx30cm print bed is a waste of energy and money.

---

4 Which printer is right for me?

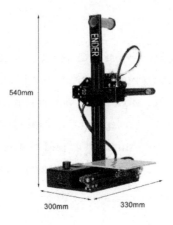

Figure 20 Creality Ender 2 compact printer

The most common printing bed sizes are given as a guide:

Small: 15 x 15 cm bed, 15 cm height (some even smaller)
Standard: approx. 20 x 20 cm bed, 25 cm height
Large: larger than 30 x 30 cm bed, 40 cm height

For those who have no personal experience but would like to get started, we recommend a 20 x 20 cm printing bed. The majority of the community has had good experiences with this. From time to time, a larger bed would be an advantage, but in 95% of cases the standard volume is sufficient. You should take into account that a print with 20 cm length and width and 25 cm height can take 1-2 days.

4.2 Frame

As mentioned above, the framework is one of the most important aspects of good printing. Therefore, it is not advisable to buy a printer that is not constructed of a rigid material such as aluminium. Most manufacturers have now also recognised this. Nevertheless, it is better to spend €30 more and buy a printer with a solid aluminium profile frame; the thicker and heavier, the more stable. Remember that you want to avoid dramatic resonance effects (see bridge collapse in 2.1, Fig. 7).

4.3 Electronics

In the case of electronics, safety is the most important consideration. For the power supply unit, for example, a fuse should be installed as a matter of course. An on/off switch is also practical so that you don't always have to unplug the cable from the socket.

Before buying, it is also advisable to read the reviews of reputable technology portals, as the electronics are usually mentioned and it is checked whether the manufacturer has made savings in the wrong place.

Regarding other aspects of the electronics, you have to look for your own requirements, for example, for the touch display and WLAN module.

4.4 Miscellaneous

As already mentioned under the general aspects of a printer, a heated printing bed is very important, especially for beginners, as it increases the adhesion of the filament. Additional functions such as an autolevel sensor or a filament change option during printing are also nice to have. In general, a lot depends on the budget. Some inexpensive printer kits are available for about €100, but have an inferior frame, immature electronics and have to be assembled by the customer (workload of about 4 - 5 hours). These were very popular a few years ago, which is why there is a huge community. From today's point of view, however, it is definitely not recommended to buy such a kit. You have to invest more money in security upgrades, spare parts and possibly missing parts that are needed for operation, so you are not actually saving money. If you have less than €200 at your disposal, try the second hand market. Just make sure that the printer is 100% functional.

4.5 An overview of the current market

When buying a new product, there are some brands that have become established. One of the first and highest quality companies in the field of 3D printing is still Prusa Research with their top model the Prusa i3 MK3, the successor of the very popular i3 MK2.

This serves as a "template" (to put it nicely) for various replicas by other companies from the Far East, such as Anet, Creality and Geeetech, which, however, have mainly positioned themselves in the low-price segment.

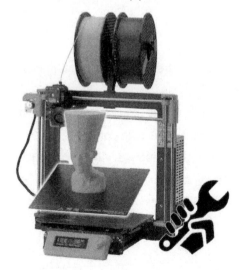

Figure 21 Prusa i3 MK3

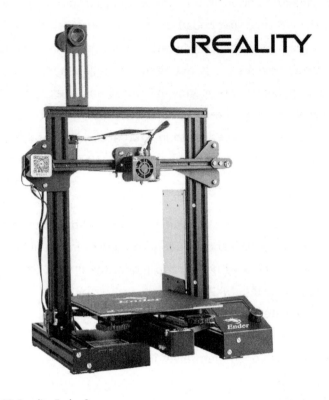

Figure 22 Creality Ender 3

In the price range around €200, for example, the Creality Ender 3 is ahead in the market, and it is basically a Prusa i3 replica.

It offers an aluminium frame, a printing volume of 22 cm in length and width and 25 cm in height and comes half-assembled. The complete assembly takes 30 minutes. There are no features such as auto-levelling or a touch display. As a clone of this clone, a Geeetech A10 for about €150 might be interesting. It is almost identical in construction, but with a low resolution display.

4 Which printer is right for me?

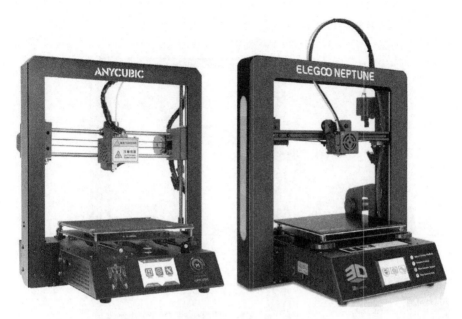

Figure 23 Anycubic i3 Mega   *Figure 24 Elegoo Neptune*

In the price range up to €300, there are only a few printers with a good price/performance ratio. The Anycubic i3 Mega is recommendable. It has a large community and all technical standards. An alternative that is somewhat cheaper is the already mentioned Elegoo Neptune. The two models are identical in many points and mimic the Prusa i3 in their mode of operation. Above all, they are visually attractive, as they both have a fairing around the Z-axis. Further advantages are a glass plate as printing bed, covered with a foil for better adhesion, as well as a 3.5-inch touch display.

The JGAURORA A1S offers a somewhat larger printing volume of 30x30x30 cm, but it clearly breaks the €300 mark. An alternative again is a Geeetech; the A20 has a printing volume of 25x25x25 cm.

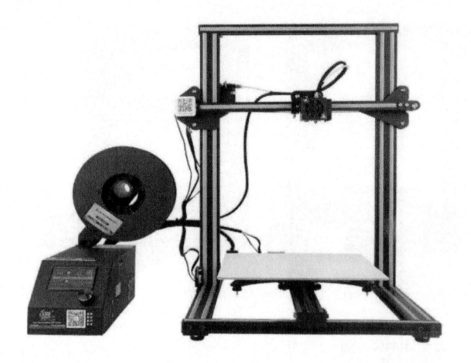

Figure 25 Creality CR-10

If you want to print larger, there is almost no way around a Creality CR10S. With a printing volume of 30x30x40 cm, it has by far the largest print space. The Anycubic Chiron offers an even larger print space with 40x40x45 cm for over €500. An alternative is also the Anet A8 Plus, with a printing volume of 30x30x35 cm. Also in the same league is the JGAURORA A5S with 30.5x30.5x32 cm or the Geeetech A30 with 32x32x42 cm.

4 Which printer is right for me?

Figure 26 Renkforce RF500

If you want to climb to the top of the 3D printers, you should look around for an original Prusa i3 MK3 or a Renkforce series printer from Conrad (up to well over €1000). The Renkforce printers in particular are at the top of the list in terms of reliability. However, the price/performance ratio is correspondingly worse. Even higher priced are printers that are mainly used in industry, for example the Ultimaker series. The Ultimaker 3 is a good €3600. However, since most newcomers are more interested in a low-cost printer, we will not go into detail about high-priced printers. In general, everything that is mentioned here is, of course, not concrete purchase advice but merely illustrations and impressions that can be confirmed by a large part of the 3D community. Before buying, you should check whether the printer really meets your requirements, read reviews or watch YouTube videos if necessary. These videos are produced in very high quality nowadays and show what is important for you.

4.6 Which filament is for the printer?

As we have already seen, PLA is recommended as a beginner's filament because it does not emit any toxic fumes and is relatively easy to process. With PLA you can get to know the principle of 3D printing and your printer, so that you can then try out other filaments such as PETG, ABS or nylon. With PLA, there are price ranges from €12 per kilogram up to €50 per kilogram. Most of them are in the range between €18 and €25. High quality brands are Janbex (approx. 23 €/kg), The Filament (approx. 22 €/kg) and to some extent Amazon Basics (under 20 €/kg). Also, Geeetech and Eryone are established brands with consistently high quality (approx. 22 €/kg).

Anything below these prices cannot be recommended. Of course, it is possible to print with cheap filaments, but especially at the beginning, the right filament can save you from unsuccessful prints, and the corresponding frustration, due to no fault of your own.

Note: All the mentioned printers need filament with 1.75 mm diameter. Absolutely pay attention to this!

To sum up, with a new printer you buy a new hobby. Setting the printer down, entering all the standard settings once and running it like this for the next few years unfortunately does not work in practice. There are many parts that move and wear out. An electronic component can give up the

4 Which printer is right for me?

ghost. But here again, there's no need to worry. A Prusa i3-style 3D printer is not rocket science, as was discussed in the previous chapters. You do not have to be a mechanical engineer to make modifications. In many forums or on YouTube, there are excellent step-by-step instructions for almost every printer model.

5. First prints

5.1 From idea to machine code

After you've found the right printer and filament for your needs, it's time for the practical part.

People who buy a 3D printer are usually very creative. Who doesn't like the idea of being able to transform their idea of an object into a tangible sculpture? Spare parts, gifts, gadgets – there are no limits to your creativity. It is recommended to proceed systematically.
Before a figure can be printed, the idea must first be converted into a computer simulation, a 3D model.

> Computer-aided design (CAD) programs are used to create digital 3D models.

Microsoft Windows already offers simple programs for this purpose, such as the Windows 3D Builder. This is suitable for beginners, for example to design simple blocks or small, simple shapes and parts. However, it is not possible to create realistic facial features or filigree elements. For small spare parts or simple shapes like gears or similar, there is software like FreeCad, 123D Design or Tinkercad. In the hobby area, the software Fusion 360, with which you can create complex technical models, has established itself to a large extent.
There is also CAD software for professional use, for example by film studios. These are often expensive and difficult to learn.

This guide uses existing 3D models, which you can use if you want to start

5. First prints

printing right away. The 3D printing community has already created many models and is happy to share them. You can search for existing 3D models on websites like thingiverse.com, youmagine.com, pinshape.com or cults3d.com. Please note that depending on the object, the files may only be downloadable after paying a fee or registering. A big advantage of thingiverse.com is that all models can be downloaded free of charge – note that commercial use is generally not allowed. In addition, you can also find very complex models, some of them by professional designers.

After you have found and downloaded a suitable model, you have to prepare the model for the 3D printer.

As an example for this guide, the object "Owl statue" by the user "cushwa" is used. The very popular model of an owl on a tree trunk can be found at https://www.thingiverse.com/thing:18218.

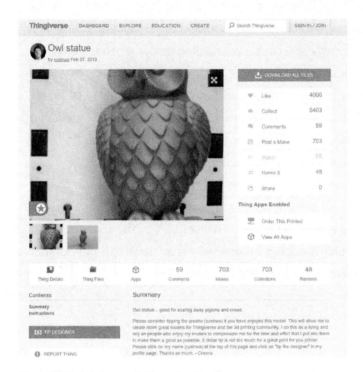

Figure 27 Owl statue model from "cushwa"

After all files have been downloaded and unzipped, you will find (next to the folder with pictures and description) the 3D model of the owl in stl format in the folder "files". Now you only have to prepare it for printing.

> The 3D printer is a relatively "stupid" machine that only executes machine commands called G-codes, so you need a program that creates a list of machine commands adapted to the printer from the 3D model.

Programs that generate G-code are known as "slicers". There, you enter your 3D model, set a few points such as temperature or printing speed and get the finished G-code file which the printer can process further. Well-known slicer programs include Ultimakers Cura, Simplify3D, Octoprint,

5. First prints

Sl3cer and many more.

The free software Cura is recommended as a beginner program, as it already has many printer profiles saved, meaning the settings for a 3D printer, and contains many additional functions and setting options.

In addition, Cura is also used by a large part of the community, so quick help can be found there if you have questions.

The latest version can be downloaded at https://ultimaker.com/en/products/ultimaker-cura-software. After installing Cura, you will need to enter the settings for your printer. As mentioned above, many known printer profiles are already stored. If your printer is not included, you can enter the necessary data such as print bed size under "Custom".

The Elegoo Neptune is used as an example printer. Although there is already a default setting for the Elegoo Neptune model, a new custom profile is created for illustration purposes. The printer has a printing volume of 20.5 x 20.5 cm (in Cura everything is entered in mm, so 205 x 205 mm). The printer also has a heated bed and a nozzle with a diameter of 0.4 mm. The filament diameter under "Extruder" should be 1.75 mm. The default setting here is 2.85 mm, so make sure you change it! Once the printer profile has been created, you will be taken to the main screen of Cura. If you want to change the language in Cura to German, go to Preferences -> configure Cura -> General -> Language. Cura must be restarted afterwards.

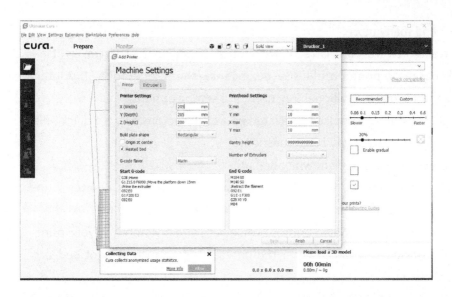

Figure 28 Setting the profile

Most of the printer's success depends on the settings, not the printer itself.
Therefore, it is important to know the possible settings and their effects.
First, you should have a basic understanding of how an object is printed.

5. First prints

Cura divides the object into layers and calculates the travel path of the print head for each layer. Since making an object out of solid material (without hollows) would be a huge waste of filament and would increase the printing time, all slicer programs create a hollow structure from the 3D model. They divide the object into walls, which are printed completely, and the inner area, which is not visible in the resulting print. This area is filled with a thin pattern so that instead of 100%, only 50%, 20% or even less, of the object interior is filled. This saves filament and time. Another aspect here is that the stability of an object also depends on the filling density. Accordingly, considerably more filling is used for functional parts than for figures that only serve a decorative purpose. If you look at the setting options in Cura (on the right side of the screen in the current version), you will quickly be overwhelmed. There are many settings or parameters which are not primarily required and which do not show significant differences at first glance, and others which would be important but are not shown by default. To change the settings, click on the gear wheel next to the respective category (Quality). A list with all possible settings opens, which can be activated by clicking on them.

We will systematically go through the setting options and their descriptions.

Figure 29 Difference between 0.1mm (left) and 0.2mm (right) layer thickness

QUALITY

Layer Thickness

The layer thickness indicates how thick an applied layer should be. With a thinner layer thickness, individual layers are less discernible, but the printing process takes longer.

As a guide, 0.2 mm gives a good balance of print time and quality. Layer thicknesses in the range of 0.1 mm are used for very detailed figures, and greater layer thicknesses are used for less delicate but functional parts where the visual appearance is not so important. In the illustration, for example, you can see the "staircase effect" on the ears in 0.2 mm layer thickness.

Additional option: thickness of the first layer

In contrast to wall thickness, the "thickness of the first layer" setting is only responsible for the first layer and is an important parameter. It also determines how well the print adheres to the printing bed.

With good adhesion, this value can be left at 0.2 - 0.3 mm.

5. First prints

HOUSING

Wall thickness

Here you can increase the wall thickness, which refers to the area that forms the object's housing and is filled 100%. This is especially useful when the print needs to be stabilised. Otherwise, everything can be left at standard. A wall thickness of 0.8 mm is usually sufficient for a good print and medium stability.

FILLING

Fill density

Fill density determines how much material is used and how long the print takes. For functional parts, a fill density of 40 - 80 % is recommended. For figures, 20 % is usually sufficient. This saves time as well as filament.

MATERIAL

Print temperature

The print temperature varies from filament to filament and from printer to printer and must be determined from test prints. The manufacturer's specifications cover a very wide range, for example 180 - 220°C. As a guide value for PLA, 200°C - 210°C can be used.

Additional option: print temperature of the first layer

This temperature only applies to the first layer. Afterwards, it switches to the general printing temperature. For adhesion reasons, the printing temperature of the first layer should be approx. 10°C to 20°C above the normal printing temperature. As an example, it is 220°C.

Temperature printing plate

The printing bed temperature indicates the temperature at which the printing bed is maintained during the entire printing process. This in turn is strongly dependent on the type of filament. A rough guide value for PLA is 50-60°C.

SPEED

Print speed

The print speed indicates how fast the print head or bed moves in general. The slower the speed is set, the better the print quality, but the longer it takes to print. A speed of 60 mm/s is a good average value, for smaller objects you should go down to 20-30 mm/s. Similarly, for flexible filament, a low printing speed should be selected.

Additional option: movement speed

The speed of movement indicates how fast the print head moves over blank areas to the next print point. This speed can be set much higher than the print speed, as it does not directly affect the quality of the print. However, it is important to note for which speeds the hardware of the printer, that is, the motors and guides, are designed. For example, the Elegoo Neptune allows a maximum movement speed of 100 mm/s.

Additional option: Speed of the first layer

As there are often problems with adhesion to the print, it is recommended to set the speed of the first layer to about 50% of the normal printing speed. The software developer created this option for good reason.

COOLING

If a component fan is available, here you can set how much it should cool the filament after it is extruded onto the object being built.

The preset is 100% fan speed and fits in most cases.

5. First prints

SUPPORT STRUCTURES

For certain objects, it is conceivable that the printer may have to print over-hanging walls or even start printing in the air. In order to achieve this, supports are calculated which are printed like a kind of scaffolding under the critical points and provide structural support. After printing, these structures are simply broken away. The example slicer Cura shows the critical areas to keep in red (Fig. 30). The supporting structures after the object has been made are visible in blue (Fig. 30 right).

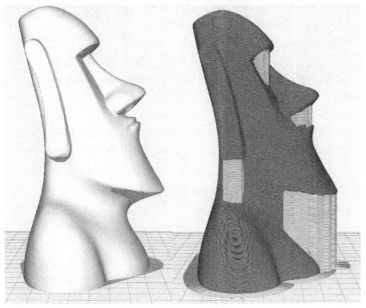

Figure 30 Supporting structures in layer view

PRINTING PLATE ADHESION

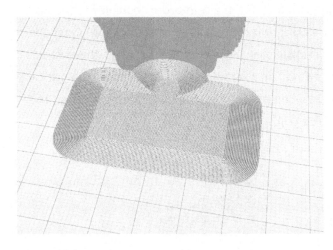

Figure 31 Brim preview

To ensure that the object adheres better to the printing bed, a border, a "brim", can be set. This can, for example, prevent the corners from coming off the printing bed (curling). If you have no adhesion problems, you can skip this point.

There is also the function "Skirt", which creates a line around the print object. This homogenises the filament flow before printing, so you get smoother flow. Since the line doesn't touch it, the actual adhesion of the print to the printing plate is not improved by this.

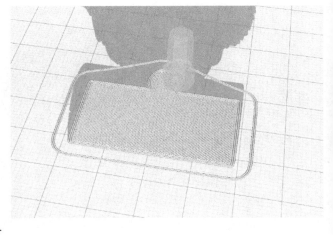

Figure 32 Skirt preview

5. First prints

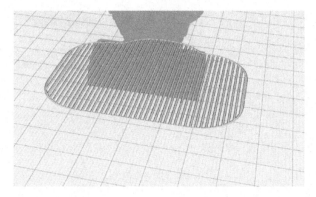

Figure 33 Raft preview

Finally, "Raft" is a function that is practical if the figure has very little contact with the printing bed, for example a ball. With "Raft", a grid is printed underneath the object to ensure even adhesion. With this, the object is lifted a few layers.

Now that you know the most important settings of the slicing program, slice the object. To do this, drag the file for the owl, for example, into the virtual installation space. The owl is loaded and you get a preview of the owl. For the settings, keep the recommended layer thickness of 0.2 mm and use 0.2 mm for "thickness of the first layer". Use the default wall thickness of 0.8 mm as well as the filling of 20%.

Next, the temperatures have to be adjusted for the filament. For PLA, a printing temperature of 200°C and bed temperature of 60°C are optimal. The printing speed should be at 60 mm/s – a good value, on average. The additional option of movement speed should be reduced to 100 mm/s.

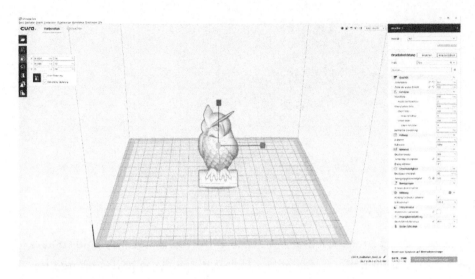

Figure 34 Cura user interface

The component fan must be activated and set to 100% for good cooling. It is recommended to activate a printing plate adhesion. In the example "Brim" was selected. The settings are now complete. Next, click on the model and you can scale it laterally with the left button. You can also adjust the size of the print. In the example, the figure has been reduced to 50% with uniform scaling (equally along the three axes).

5. First prints

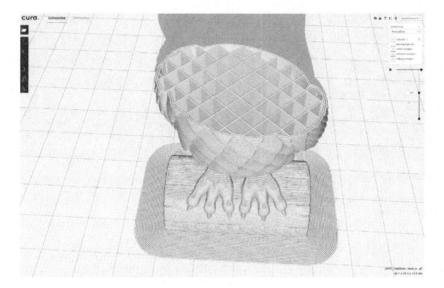

Figure 35 Preview of infill in the layer view

Now, the file can be sliced with "Prepare". This takes a few seconds, depending on the performance of the computer. If you choose "layer view" instead of "solid view" in the upper right corner, you can see how the object is built up layer by layer. You can see the Brim and the filling inside. With the slider on the side you can run through the different layers like an animation simulation. If support structures are activated, they are shown in a different colour.

Save the generated file on an SD card. After you see the message that it has been successfully saved, your first model is ready to print. Instead of saving the file to an SD card, you can send the file directly to the printer via a USB, LAN or WLAN interface.

If you open the export file in a text editor, you will see that the file consists of a sequence of machine code commands. Everything written after a semicolon is a comment that increases readability but is not a command for the 3D printer.

```
CFFFP_OwlReDo1_fixed_sc.gcode - Editor
Datei  Bearbeiten  Format  Ansicht  Hilfe
;FLAVOR:Marlin
;TIME:4750
;Filament used: 5.91291m
;Layer height: 0.2
;Generated with Cura_SteamEngine 3.6.0
M140 S60
M105
M190 S60
M104 S200
M105
M109 S200
M82 ;absolute extrusion mode
G28 ;Home
G1 Z15.0 F6000 ;Move the platform down 15mm
;Prime the extruder
G92 E0
G1 F200 E3
G92 E0
G92 E0
G1 F1500 E-6.5
;LAYER_COUNT:376
;LAYER:0
M107
G0 F3000 X79.012 Y83.916 Z0.2
;TYPE:SKIRT
G1 F1500 E0
G1 F1800 X79.634 Y83.429 E0.02627
G1 X80.301 Y83.007 E0.05253
G1 X81.008 Y82.655 E0.07879
G1 X81.747 Y82.377 E0.10506
G1 X82.668 Y82.143 E0.13666
G1 X83.288 Y82.025 E0.15765
G1 X84.07 Y81.916 E0.18391
G1 X84.742 Y81.887 E0.20629
G1 X120.723 Y81.867 E1.40302
G1 X121.511 Y81.907 E1.42926
G1 X122.164 Y82 E1.4512
G1 X122.783 Y82.116 E1.47215
G1 X123.551 Y82.301 E1.49842
G1 X124.296 Y82.562 E1.52468
G1 X125.011 Y82.898 E1.55095
```

Figure 36 Excerpt from GCODE file

This gives the software (Marlin), the calculated time TIME:4750 (seconds) and, further down, G28 ;HOME, which is the machine command for homing, that is, moving back the axes before starting printing.

5. First prints

5.2 From machine code to 3D printing

Before you print, the printer must be set up and connected. For each model, this is slightly different. Most modern 3D printers come semi-assembled, for more economical transport, and you only have to screw together some parts of the frame that are not mounted. If you use a kit or build it yourself, the assembly takes longer, so for beginners a partly or completely assembled printer is recommended.

Once the printer is set up, connect the cabling. The instructions and reverse polarity protected plugs make it possible even for a layman without extensive knowledge of electronics to wire the printer correctly. It is also advisable, if the manufacturer has not already taken extra measures, to fasten all long cables that do not need to move during operation so that they do not get in the way of the moving parts. Use cable ties or, later, when the printer is running the way you want, something more elegant with 3D printed brackets.

If the electronics are properly connected and the printer receives power, you can bring it to life for the first time. You can work your way through the menu using a rotating control knob or, where applicable, via touch. Most menus are very intuitive and user-friendly. Once you have moved all axes back and forth and gotten over the initial wonder, you can start preparing for the first print. The first step is levelling the print bed.

Manual levelling:

The aim of levelling is to ensure that the nozzle is at the correct distance from the heating bed.

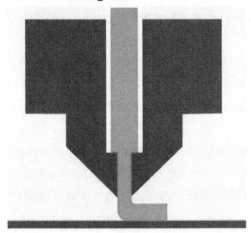

Figure 37 Nozzle too far from the print bed

If the nozzle is too far from the heating bed, too little pressure is exerted on the filament. It has no or only poor adhesion. The corners or the whole print can come loose.

5. First prints

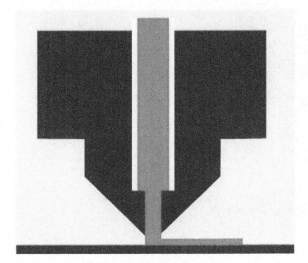

Figure 39 Nozzle too close to the printing bed

If the printing bed is levelled too high or the nozzle is too close to the bed, the filament cannot exit properly and the filament flow is impaired. This can damage the bed or the extruder motor, for example, if it has to push the filament against the increased resistance.

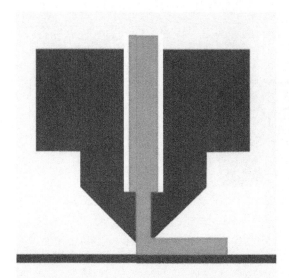

Figure 38 Correct distance from nozzle to heating bed

The bed is correctly levelled when the filament has enough pressure on the bed without interrupting the flow of the filament. This gives the best adhesion and therefore the best results.

It is therefore important to make sure that the bed is neither too high nor too low. But how exactly do you level the bed?

Figure 40 Manual levelling using thermal paper

Out of the box, the printing bed is probably not perfectly aligned with the axes. The mounted knurled screws can be turned to raise or lower the corners of the printing bed. You should proceed systematically:

First, screw all the way in all screws or wheels of the printing bed so that the bed is in the lowest position. Next, preheat the bed to the desired printing temperature. With PLA, for example, this is 60°C. Then, select the home function in the printer menu. This is usually called "Home All", "Auto Home", or "Move all axes back". Some printers already support a level function by the software. If this is available, you can select level there. In this case, the printer will also move to the home position first. Next, place a very thin sheet of paper between the heating bed and the nozzle. Thermal paper is best for this purpose, for example an old sales slip. If necessary, however, thin printing paper is also sufficient. Then, move the print head to the middle of the heating bed. With a 200 x 200 mm heating bed, this would be point: X = 100 mm and Y = 100 mm. Next, lower the Z-axis to Z = 0 mm. Then, unscrew all wheels evenly until there is so little space between the thermal paper and the nozzle that you feel a slight resistance when moving the paper. If the thermal paper cannot be moved at all, it was too much and you have to tighten all screws again a little bit (lower the bed). If the pressure is too light, you have to loosen the screws accordingly. Often, the knurled screws indicate which direction to turn to raise or lower the bed. This may have to be repeated until roughly the right height is reached.

Next comes the fine adjustment. To do this, each corner is moved one after the other by adjusting the respective screw so that the height creates slight resistance on the paper in between. The test points should be about 1 - 2 cm from the edge of the printing bed. As an example, the positions for a 200 x 200 mm print bed are:

front left: X = 10 mm, Y = 10 mm

front right: X = 190 mm, Y = 10 mm

back left: X = 10 mm, Y = 190 mm

back right: X = 190 mm, Y = 190 mm

Repeat until all corners are checked and all points are correct. This can take some time, but for a clean print, especially the adhesion and the first layer, it is important that the bed is levelled properly.

Levelling with auto-level sensor:

If the printer already has an auto-level sensor installed, you only need to enter the Z offset, which is the difference in height between the sensor and

5. First prints

the nozzle. If the sensor is triggered and the nozzle is 1 mm from the print bed, the offset is -1 mm. In order to determine this offset, you must first "home" again and move the print head over the bed, preferably in the middle. Here too, the bed must be heated up and thermal paper is again required. Then, the head is lowered until a resistance is felt on the thermal paper, just like with normal levelling without an auto-level sensor. However, the bed is not raised by means of knurled screws, but rather the print head is lowered via the motion control.

If the correct point is found, the print head is at $Z = -1.7$ mm, for example. This is then the Z-offset you are looking for. You can usually enter this in the settings under "Z-Offset". Please note that the value is negative, therefore -1.7 mm is entered, not 1.7 mm!

Now, the print bed is levelled and the printer is fully prepared. After inserting the SD card, the G-code file can be selected under "Print". The printer will first preheat the heating bed to the set temperature, in the example to 60°C. Depending on the model and temperature, this takes two to five minutes. Then, the nozzle is heated and printing begins. After about one hour and 20 minutes, the first print will be completed. If something doesn't work as desired, it's not so bad, because almost nobody does it right the first time.

6. Maintenance and wear

For a 3D printer, especially a lower price one, maintenance needs to be done at regular intervals. This not only saves on hardware replacements, the printer lasts longer and the print results remain consistently good. Most components should be cared for as needed and within a fixed time. The following time intervals are therefore only a rough guide. If the printer is moved, rebuilt, etc., you will have to do the maintenance accordingly earlier.

We'll start with the daily maintenance tasks.

6.1 Daily maintenance:

Dust and filament residues

- Before each print, the printer should be cleaned of dust and filament residues from previous prints (or failures). If care is neglected, dust and filament residues can accumulate, for example on the mainboard or the fans, and in the worst case, lead to overheating and failure of the cooling system.

6.2 Weekly maintenance:

Cleaning the printing bed

- In order to keep the adhesion constantly high and to make the print bed surface more durable, it is recommended to clean the bed of grease and other residues approximately once a week. Do not use cleaners that are too aggressive, as these can attack the sensitive coating of the printing bed. In most cases, warm water and a mild detergent are sufficient.

6. Maintenance and wear

- Cleaning the nozzle

- The nozzle gets dirty over time, so the nozzle should be heated once a week and, with the help of a nozzle cleaner (available for a few euros), cleaned both inside and out. At the same time, check the degree of wear on the nozzle.

6.3 Monthly maintenance:

General cleaning of the printer
- The printer should be thoroughly cleaned approximately once a month. This means that all axes and guides are cleaned and freed from dust and impurities. The degree of wear, for example of the bearings, can also be checked during this process.

Update firmware
It is worth checking once a month whether the firmware of the printer and the version of the slicer are still up-to-date. Most of the time you can find the information directly on the website of the manufacturer or distributor.

Cleaning the extruder
- Especially for extruders with a closed design, the cover should be removed and filament residues should be scraped off with a brush. This prevents the filament from slipping through due to insufficient adhesion to the extruder gear wheel.

Check cables
- As a safety measure, you should check at least once a month

whether all cables of the motors, the heating bed, the sensors and hotends are still intact. The insulation of the moving cables can rub against the frame if they are not fixed properly.

6.4 Maintenance every 3 - 6 months:

Clean hotend

- Depending on the printer's degree of utilisation, it is recommended to clean the entire hot end from time to time. Take the hot end completely apart, separate its individual parts and remove any filament that may have seized up on or inside the heating block and the nozzle. Due to the constant heating and cooling, deposits can accumulate inside the hotend, which can lead to clogging of the hotend. The PTFE tube can also be checked during this process.

Check belt tension

- The belt can stretch out over time. The constant movement stretches it out or makes small holes. Here too, regular maintenance and checking for wear and tear is advantageous for ordering a replacement belt in good time.

Lubrication of the guides

- The Z threaded spindle rods and the X and Y axis guides should be lubricated with sewing machine oil. Frequent use requires shorter intervals between oilings.

-

6.5 Further tips for long-lasting printing fun

The filament rolls must be stored in a cool and dry place. The reason for this is that many filaments, such as nylon or PETG, draw humidity from the air and bind it to themselves. When the filament is subsequently processed, the water adhering to the filament vaporises and deteriorates the print image. Some filaments such as PLA are not affected much by this. Others such as nylon are very strongly and should be dried after long-time storage or, even better, stored in airtight boxes with desiccant packs (with silica beads, for example).

If you do not plan on printing for several days, pull the filament out of the hotend and roll it up. The hotend can be spot cleaned and any filament residues can be removed. If the filament contains additives such as wood or metal particles, the filament should be pulled out of the hotend after each print so that the particles cannot solidify in the hotend.

6.6 Spare parts

If a print object is needed at short notice, such as a personalised birthday present, then a sudden failure of the 3D printer could be a catastrophe. Ordering spare parts would take too long and there are hardly any specialist shops for 3D printers. The only option is to prepare for a failure in advance.

After all, despite all the care and maintenance taken, sooner or later parts of the printer will show signs of wear and will have to be replaced. If the failure happens during a print run, this may be unpleasant, but if you then have no spare parts on hand and have to wait another few days for suitable parts, this is particularly annoying, so it is advisable to always have the following parts in stock.

Nozzles:
It happens from time to time that the nozzle accidentally scratches the heating bed, becomes blocked or simply wears out over time. It is therefore advisable to always have a few spare nozzles at hand. Almost all printers use standard brass nozzles with 0.2 to 1mm orifices. Even if the nozzles are vis-

ually different, most nozzles fit on an M6 thread heating block. These are available on websites such as Aliexpress or Ebay directly from the Far East for sometimes 50 cents a piece. Delivery times are sometimes very long (2 - 6 weeks), so order early. Of course, these nozzles are not all that is out there.

Figure 41 Spare nozzles from 0.2mm to 1.0mm

Alternatively, there are European distributors like *E3D*, which are much more expensive (about 10€ per nozzle), but consistently deliver good quality.

It should be noted that after nozzle replacement, as with any alteration, the printing bed must be re-levelled.

Straps:

Just as quickly as a nozzle can become clogged, a belt can give out, move out of place or become porous. It is therefore advisable to always have a

6. Maintenance and wear

few metres of replacement belt at hand to get back to printing as soon as possible.

Stock/rolls:
The moving parts of the printer are the most vulnerable, so it is advisable to take precautions in good time. Most printers use linear ball bearings like LM8LUU (including Anycubic i3 Mega) or roller bearings like 625ZZ (such as the Ender 3, the Geeetech A series or a hybrid like the Elegoo Neptune).
Especially for the bearings, you should consider quality parts made in Germany instead of relying on cheap wares from China. Although these cost considerably more, they are also more durable. Either way, you should always have a few replacement bearings in storage.

Now that the largest potential sources of failure have been given, we will discuss some problems that might occur, especially for beginners, which can cause headaches.
The following chapter covers the 10 most common causes of errors and how to deal with them.

7. The most frequent causes of errors

It would be too good if no problems ever arose while 3D printing. In this guide, we have already explained some of the causes and consequences associated with these. A list of the problems that many beginners have to experience at the beginning will be discussed in more detail here. Here are the top 10 entry-level problems in 3D printing:

7.1 No filament comes out of the nozzle

Description:
No filament flows out of the nozzle, although it is hot and filament has been inserted.

Cause:
Something along the way from the extruder motor to the nozzle opening is blocked or the extruder motor is faulty.
If the motor does not rotate, it is defective or a cable is not properly connected. In rare cases, the mainboard may be the cause.
Does the motor turn, try to push the filament and clatter? If this happens, the nozzle or supply line is blocked by dirt, charred material or something else. Filament of inferior quality or with a diameter that is too thick or varies greatly can also cause or intensify this effect.

Solution:
Check all cables and connections. Refer to the printer's manual for the connections of the extruder. If this is not the problem, cleaning the print head or replacing the nozzle will help.

7.2 The object comes loose during printing

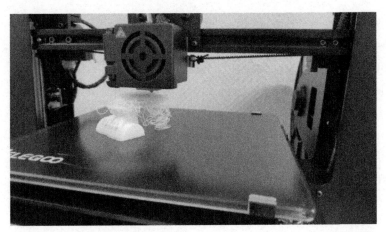

Figure 42 Print detaches from the bed

Description:

The first layer of filament does not stick to the printing bed or the object loosens during printing, resulting in a single ball of filament.

Cause:

The printer processes plastics that expand when heated and contract when cooled. This means that if the filament cools from 210°C or above to bed temperature within seconds, it contracts. The warping depends on the printing material (see chapter 3). If the adhesion to the bed is not strong enough to hold the filament to the heating bed, the print will release. Over time, the coating of the printing bed will also wear off and the adhesion will decrease.

Solution:

The bed must be levelled lower. You can also reduce the thickness of the first layer a little so that it becomes very thin. A thickness of 0.1 - 0.2 mm is good for the first layer, no matter how thick the general layer thickness is set.

It is also recommended to increase the temperature of the first layer and the general heating bed temperature by a few degrees. With PLA, instead of the standard 50 - 60°C, it is also possible to increase the temperature to 70 - 75°C. It may also be better to reduce the printing speed of the first layer, for example down to 15 mm/s.

The printing bed adhesion must also be increased, for example by using a new printing bed foil. More rudimentary solutions, such as applying painter's tape or adhesive, can also improve adhesion.

7.3 The corners of the print come loose - Warping

Figure 43 The corners of the print lift up

Description:

7. The most frequent causes of errors

The first layer looks good, but after the next layers have been printed, you can see that the corners or whole parts of the print lift off the bed.

Cause:
The same phenomenon as in the second point, but not as pronounced. The print sticks to the print bed, but as the filament cools, the weakest points, and these are usually the corners, are detached from the print bed.

Solution:
The same steps must be taken here as described in the second point. Either improve the adhesion, level the bed lower or slow down the cooling, for example by increasing the temperature of the printing bed. In most cases, however, there is an adhesion problem due to an incorrectly levelled printing bed. The Brim function described in chapter 5.1, which has been set up for exactly this scenario, provides a remedy with the setting of an 8-mm Brim.

7.4 Holes in print - (partial) under-extrusion

Figure 44 Holes in the surface

Description:

The print is brittle, perforated and has gaps either in certain places or everywhere or only on the sides, top or bottom.

Cause:

Too little filament comes through the nozzle, which means that too little material is applied and holes or leaks occur. This is therefore referred to as under-extrusion of the material.

Either the extruder does not feed or cannot feed enough filament or the

7. **The most** frequent causes of errors

nozzle does not put out enough material (may be clogged).

If the problem is only on the upper and lower surfaces, these are set too thin.

Solution:

First, check whether it is a software or a hardware problem.

Is the diameter of the filament set to 1.75 mm? In Cura, you can find this under Configuration-> Printer -> Manage printer -> Device settings -> Extruder 1.

Also, set "Material -> Flow" to 100 % and make sure that the nozzle is set to the correct diameter (usually 0.4 mm).

If everything is set correctly there, the heat of the nozzle may not be sufficient to melt the filament fast enough. In this case, it helps to increase the temperature of the nozzle and reduce the speed. If this does not help either, the nozzle is clogged or blocked. In this case, cleaning or replacing the nozzle will help.

If the holes only occur in the upper or lower layers, the thickness of the upper/lower layer must be increased. A good value is then 4 - 5 of the layers. You can also increase the infill, as this supports the upper layers.

Changing other settings might help such as reducing the line width or increasing the overlap of two lines.

7.5 Too much material – over-extrusion

Figure 45 Over-extrusion

Description:

The outer lines are spongy, the walls have excessively large grooves/bumps or the details are blurred.

Cause:

In contrast to under-extrusion, too much filament is extruded. As a result, the excess filament is pressed out at the sides and unsightly bulbous structures (plops) are created.   This is called over-extrusion of the material.

Solution:

Over-extrusion is the opposite of under-extrusion. The flow must be set to 100%, and the filament diameter must not be too small. Furthermore, an incorrectly entered nozzle diameter could be the cause. See Configuration-> Printer -> Manage printers -> Device settings -> Extruder. If this does not help, the flow must be manually reduced. It is recommended to go down in steps of 5% until the print image improves.

7.6 Printing has offset (layer shifting)

Figure 46 Offset in X direction

Description:
The model has offsets or is shifted in some places.

Cause:
This is almost always a mechanical problem. Something prevents the axle from moving for a short time. This could be loose cables or too much friction or maybe a deflection pulley turns with difficulty. In rare cases, the electronics (stepper motor driver) may be at fault, for example because the motors or drivers overheat and lose steps.

Solution:

Check whether the axes are stiff, whether they are perfectly aligned or whether something is obstructing the axes during printing. If steps are lost because the motors are too weak, it helps to reduce the printing speed or slightly increase the motor drive voltage.

7.7 Thread formation (stringing)

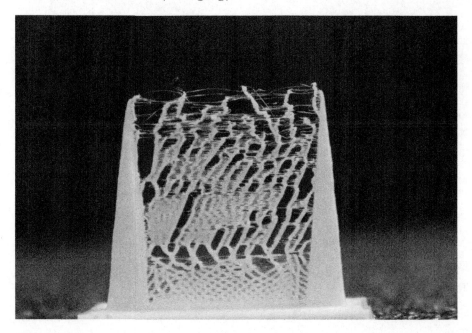

Figure 47 Stringing

Description:

Threads are pulled between two points, although there should be no material there.

7. The most frequent causes of errors

Cause:

When moving the print head over what are actually empty areas, the still liquid material runs out of the nozzle and pulls into threads. The filament is too hot and simply pours out.

Solution:

With most slicers, you can set a retraction so that the extruder pulls the filament back before it passes over empty areas. In Cura, this is an additional function under the category "material". You can increase the draw-in distance and speed. If there is major stringing, the temperature of the heating block can be reduced by 5-10°C.

7.8 You can see the filling lines on the outer walls

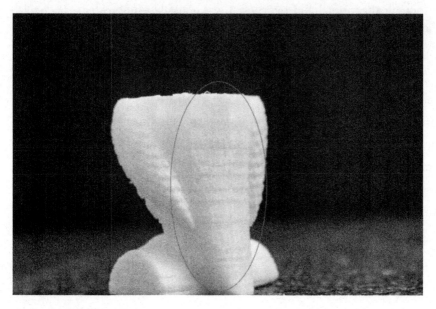

Figure 48 Visible infill artefacts

Description:

On the outer walls, the starting points of the infill are visible. Regular patterns can be seen on the outer walls.

Cause:

The outer walls are too thin – that is why there is more filament at the points where the infill lines meet the wall than at the other points.

Solution:

It is necessary to increase the number of external walls. In Cura, these are set to 2 as standard, so increasing them to 3 or 4 should help. If necessary, you can also reduce the infill speed and the wall speed so that the nozzle can smoothen the transitions.

7. The most frequent causes of errors

7.9. Bulging corners - elephant foot

Figure 49 Elephant foot

Description:

The print has unsightly accumulations of filament at the corners. The edges are not straight.

Cause:

The hot filament does not cool down fast enough and runs off. The weight of the object additionally pushes the still viscous filament downwards. Like with warping, the material contracts, but the adhesion to the printing bed is strong enough that the corners do not come loose. However, unsightly deformations occur.

Solution:

Reducing the printing temperature, the temperature of the first layers and the heating bed should help. However, a compromise must always be found between good plate adhesion and avoiding elephant feet. If the temperature is too low, you risk warping or lifting of the print. If the temperature is too high, the elephant feet described will occur. Levelling the printing bed can also help here.

7.10. The printing bed cannot be levelled

Description:

The printing bed is significantly higher on one side than on the other. Even if the set screws are completely tightened on one side and completely un-screwed on the opposite side, the nozzle is not at the same distance from the print bed at all points.

Cause:

The X-axis itself is inclined, or the axis is suspended higher on one side than on the other. This is a mechanical problem. If it occurs more often, one motor rotates slower than the other, so the motor or motor driver is defective.

Solution:

Deactivate the motors with the software and disconnect the cable of the Z-motors. Carefully(!) turn the motors by hand so that the lower side is lifted. Then, reconnect and test everything. If the problem persists, repeat the procedure.

On almost all printers, you can also adjust the height of the Z-end stop if the nozzle is generally too far from the print bed.

8th bonus chapter – Gift idea: Lithophane pictures

8.1 Lithophanes – what, how, why?

Before describing the actual printing of a lithophane, there are various terms that you should know. What is lithophany anyway?

Lithophany describes the art or the technique of presenting the relief of an object. A lithophane, on the other hand, is the concrete realisation, for example the picture made. The word "lithophane" is derived, like so many technical terms, from the ancient Greek word *lithos* "stone "and *phainein* "make appear". The art of lithophany is older than you might think. The first patent was issued in Paris in 1827. At that time of course, lithophanes were not printed by a 3D printer, but carved in porcelain. Now, you can make a comparable work of art using a different skill set. Example of a lithophane image from a 3D printer:

Figure 50 Lithophane unlit

The picture of the print without backlighting already gives you an idea of the outline, but the effect is only impressive when the picture is lit from behind:

Figure 51 Lithophane when lit

Lithophane pictures are perfect as gifts or for decoration. Each Lithophane is unique and individual. You can immortalise almost any picture. Lithophane pictures can have a very high resolution and can be illuminated by any imaginable light source, from sunlight to LEDs.

But how do you get a file from a normal picture that can be printed and illuminated? There are programs where you can simply upload the picture and get a file back for 3D printing a lithophane. There's no magic in these programs, only simple calculations. If you're not interested in how they work, you can skip this section and go straight to the next section, the actual printing preparation and printing.

The way these programs convert your picture into a printable relief is relatively simple. First, the image that you selected to convert is registered.

Then, the colour channels are removed so that only a monochrome image remains (this is the first step, even with lithophane software, that goes unnoticed by the user).

The most rudimentary but, at the same time, qualitatively worst method is to take the colour out of the picture. This is done by adding up the values for red, green and blue and dividing by three:

$$grey\ value = \frac{R+G+B}{3}$$

This principle is used in image processing programs, for example, if you simply set the saturation slider to 0.

A better approach is a "weighted greyscale conversion". This takes into account the fact that the human eye is more sensitive to certain colour components than to others. For example, a light-intensive green is perceived more clearly than comparable values of blue or red. With the weighted greyscale conversion, the grey value is calculated:

$$grey\ value = \frac{0.21R+0.72G+0.07B}{3}$$

This transformation is usually used in programs when converting a coloured image into greyscale.

The lower (modal) grey value, the brightness intensity, is then used to assign a thickness to the image. This is used to ensure that the illuminated object later transmits more light in the thinner areas, thus creating the relief effect.

The image is assumed to fill an 8-bit grey area; each pixel has a value from 0 (completely black) to a maximum of 255 (white). Now, the maximum and minimum thickness of the lithophane must be specified. The program calculates the corresponding wall thickness for each pixel.

It should be noted that a thicker filament wall allows less light to pass through, so the following values are assumed:

Minimum thickness: 0.8mm

Maximum thickness: 3mm.

So the value 0 for black is mapped to 3mm and the value 255 (white) is mapped to 0.8mm. Everything in between corresponds to a linear transformation.

So in our case:

$$thickness = 3mm - \frac{(3mm - 0.8mm)}{255} * grey\ value.$$

8.2 Actual creation:

Choosing the right image and preparation:

Now that you know how lithophany works, the next step is to create an actual lithophane.

In principle, you can use any picture and it will come out more or less good. But if you have several pictures to choose from, choosing the right one can improve the effect with backlighting significantly. Especially well suited are pictures that cover a high brightness spectrum and are very rich in contrast. With high contrast, the lithophane effect comes out best.

Preparing the image is not a must, but you can improve the result by a lot. Most importantly, during preparation you can quickly see whether the image is suitable for 3D printing. So the first step should be the conversion to greyscale (do not simply remove colour saturation). The difference is not big, but it is visible. You can already see from the monochrome image whether it is well suited for lithophane printing.

The contrast can then be increased or a manual black level adjustment (possibly called automatic tonal value correction) can be made using professional software. Sharpness and resolution should be maintained or could even be reduced to minimise image noise.

The right filament

The right filament can make a big difference. In principle, there are no restrictions when choosing the material. PLA is the easiest to print. With PLA, you can create the lithophane effect fairly well thanks to its high resolution and low layer thickness. Sometimes, however, the material should also be heat-resistant, for example when printing a lampshade or a tea light holder. For heat-resistant projects, PETG or ABS are recommended, even if the lithophane effect is slightly worse. For the general filament colour, white or other light shades such as beige, light blue, etc., are recommended and transparent filament is not recommended.

Orientation on the printing bed:

It is important to print the lithophane object to stand on edge and not be lying down. This does not seem plausible at first, but the printer has a much higher resolution in the x and y direction than in the z direction and there is the possibility of curving the entire motif. If it is printed lying down, a curvature is impossible due to the necessary support.

The result when printed standing is noticeably better. There are also recommendations to print the lithophane along the Y-axis. My personal experiments have not shown any qualitative difference.

The software

8th bonus chapter – Gift idea: Lithophane pictures

There are many different programs that can be used to convert an image into an STL file. The easiest way is to import the image into Cura, but it is recommended to use an external solution to convert the image. The best and probably best known website is http://3dp.rocks/lithophane/.
This website is easy to use and is available free of charge. Detailed instructions on how to set it up can be found there.
The most important setting is to set the image to "positive" under "Image Settings".

Besides these, there are many additional options, like an optional border or the possibility to adjust how many vectors are used to calculate a pixel. The settings for the cat image:

Figure1 3dp.rocks settings for cat lithophane

To enable the lithophane to stand without additional supports, "Outer Curve" is selected. The file that you generate clarifies the orientation.

Figure2 Preview of curved lithophane

The file can be downloaded and inserted into the slicer. The last step before printing is to make the following settings.

Slicer settings:
This is where it is decided how well the lithophane effect works, and whether stripes or plops or the like will appear in the picture. The settings are explained for Cura but are identical or similar for many slicers. Generally speaking, printing a lithophane requires a very high degree of precision from the printer. Therefore, before printing lithophanes, it is advisable to check

carefully that all belts are tensioned and that all carriages are smooth-running and straightened. We will now go through the most important settings:

Coating thickness:

One thing is clear: the thinner the layer thickness is, the less you can see the individual layers. But you don't have to overdo it. A thickness of 0.1 - 0.2 mm is perfectly fine. For smaller lithophanes, use 0.12 mm, and for thicker layers, 0.2 mm. It's often written that you have to set a multiple of the "golden number" (for most printers 0.4mm) of the printer. A big difference will not be noticed in practice. In the example, a layer thickness of 0.12mm is used.

Thickness of the outer wall:

The lithophane must be printed completely solid, that is, 100% filled. This can either be guaranteed with completely normal outer wall parameters and 100% infill or with correspondingly thick walls. The advantage of the second method is that the printer does not vibrate. There is no risk that the print object can detach from the print bed or that the print becomes less accurate.

It is also advisable to activate the function "compensation of wall" (name in Cura, similar in other slicers). In the example, 10 outer walls are set. This is more than sufficient.

Infill:

The parameter is irrelevant for this type of 3D printing. Since only walls are printed for the Lithophane, 0%, 50%, 99% or 100% will not give different results for the G-code

8th bonus chapter – Gift idea: Lithophane pictures

Speed:

Speed is a very important parameter. Generally, lithophanes must be printed very slowly. A general recommendation is difficult to give. It depends on the absolute size of the lithophane. A speed of 20 – 40 mm/s is a guide value. It is important to adjust the outside wall speed. In most slicers, this value is half the printing speed by default. However, since only walls are printed, the wall speed is the "normal" printing speed. For the example lithophane, 20 mm/s was used.

Adhesion assistance:

Especially with thin, curved lithophanes, it is recommended to apply a brim to improve adhesion. If the printing plate is not perfectly flat or already shows clear signs of use, a raft (see 5.1, bottom grid) can be printed instead of the brim.

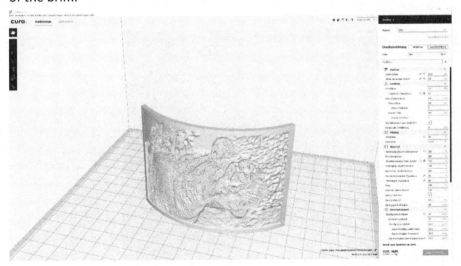

Figure3 Preview in Cura

Summary of the settings:

-0.12mm layer thickness

-10 external walls

-99% infill

-20mm/s

-Brim (alternatively raft)

-no support structures

After all settings have been made, the lithophane can be printed. Depending on its size, this can take from a few hours to a whole day. With the small 100mm example lithophane of the cat, the printing already takes h06min hours.

Various ideas can be derived from lithophane pictures. There are many other possible applications, for example printing a hollow cylinder and using it as a bedside lamp.

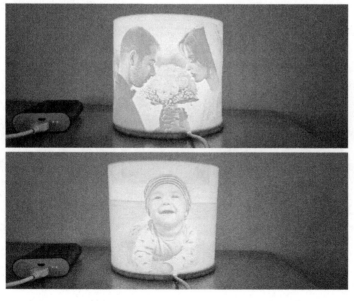

Figure4 Lithophane bedside lamp

9 Summary and outlook

In the course of this beginner's guide, basic topics such as the different manufacturing processes and the general structure of a Cartesian 3D printer were discussed. You will have noticed that the technology behind a 3D printer is not rocket science, but requires some technical understanding. Of course, it is not expected that all the details discussed in this book have been fully internalised – as they say in German, "no master has fallen from the sky yet". Nobody's first prints were perfect at the first attempt. Especially when experimenting, difficulties will arise. It is a constant learning process.

After the first model is printed, you are ready to dive further into the world of 3D printing. Cura and other slicers offer a variety of settings that still need to be explored. It's time to keep adjusting the settings to suit the printer and print many more beautiful and unique objects. Even when things don't run smoothly, the most common causes of errors can be identified and corrected.

There are no more limits to your creativity. Thingiverse and other platforms offer models for printing. It is also advisable to learn a CAD program yourself.

Picture credits:

All pictures without credit are self-produced or are available several times in relevant online shops. All pictures were taken with the permission of the copyright holder or are subject to the Creative Common License **https://creativecommons.org/licenses/?lang=de.**

Figure 1 Additive 3D printing of concrete Photo by Ricardo Gomez Angel on Unsplash

Figure 2 Cartesian 3D printer https://3d-drucker-portal.de/produkt/geeetech-a10-kaufen/

Figure 3 Polar 3D printer https://3druck.com/drucker-und-produkte/polar-3d-3d-drucken-mittels-polarkoordinaten-0329906/

Figure 4 Delta 3D printer

Figure 5 Elegoo Neptune Front https://www.amazon.de/gp/product/B07MX8B3WY

Figure 6 Standard 20x20mm aluminium profile https://aluprofile24.de/product_info.php?info=p2_strebenprofil-20x20-nut-6---zuschnitt.html

Figure 7 Collapse of the Tacoma Narrows Bridge https://www.rnz.de/panorama/magazin_artikel,-Magazin-Der-Wind-der-Wind-_arid,139578.html

Figure 8 Mainboard with pluggable drivers and ATMega2560 chip

Figure 9 ATMEGA2560 microprocessor https://pixabay.com/de/photos/arduino-atmega2560-mikrochip-2233042/

As the figure 10 Nema17 stepper motor https://de.wikipedia.org/wiki/Datei:Schrittmotorfoto.jpg

Figure 11 Schematic structure of a stepper motor https://www.motioncontroltips.com/faq-what-are-stepper-drives-and-how-do-they-work/

Figure 12 Comparison stepper motor control https://www.youtube.com/watch?v=Q0sJIGh9WNY

Abbildung 13 TMC2208 Chip https://www.trinamic.com/products/integrated-circuits/details/tmc2208-la/

Figure 14 FYSET TMC2208 Setting the driver https://wiki.fysetc.com/TMC2208/

Figure 15 Print head with and without cover

Figure 16 The structure of a 3D printer hootends - Info graphic by Sercan Kahraman, CC-BY-SA; source: threedom.de

Figure 17 Extruder motor with BMG attachment

Figure 18 Bowden and Direct Drive

Figure 19 Example of a pressurised dwelling https://box3d.eu/shop/

Figure 20 Creality Ender 2 compact printer

Figure 21 Prusa i3 mk3

Figure 22 Creality Ender 3

Figure 23 Anycubic i3 Mega Figure 24 Elegoo Neptune

Figure 25 Creality CR-10

Figure 26 Renkforce RF500

Figure 27 Owl statue of cushwa

Figure 28 Placing the profile

Figure 29Difference 0.1mm / 0.2mm layer thickness

Figure 30 Supporting structures in the layer view

Figure 31 Brim preview

Figure 32 Skrit preview

Figure 33 Raft preview

Figure 34 Cura user interface

Figure 35Preview infill in the layer view

Figure 36 Extract from GCODE file

Figure 37 Nozzle too far from the print bed

Figure 38 Correct distance from nozzle to heating bed

Figure 39 Nozzle too close to the printing bed

Figure 40 Manual levelling using thermal paper

Figure 41Replacement nozzles 0.2mm to 1.0mm https://de.aliexpress.com/item/32820351770

Figure 42Print detaches from bed

Figure 43 The corners of the print lift up

Figure 44 Holes in the surface

Figure 45 Overextrusion

Figure 46 Offset in X direction

Figure 47 Stringing

Figure 48 Visible infill artefacts

Figure 49 Elephant foot

About the author

Benjamin Spahic was born in Heidelberg, Germany in 1995 and grew up in a village of 8,000 souls near Karlsruhe, Germany. His passion for technology is reflected in his studies of electrical engineering with focus on information technology at the University of Applied Sciences in Karlsruhe.

Afterwards he deepened his knowledge in the field of regenerative energy production at the Karlsruhe University of Applied Sciences.

Free eBook:

To do this, send a message with the subject "3D printing EN", as well as a screenshot of the purchase or proof of order from Amazon to the email:

Benjamin-Spahic@web.de

I will send you the eBook immediately.

If you are missing something, did not like something or you have suggestions for improvement or questions, please send me an e-mail.

Constructive criticism is important to be able to improve something. I am constantly revising the book and am happy to respond to any constructive suggestions for improvement.

Otherwise, if you liked the book, I would also appreciate a positive review on Amazon. This helps the visibility of the book and is the biggest praise an author can get.

Your Benjamin

Imprint:

Author: Benjamin Spahic
Address:
Benjamin Spahic
Konradin-Kreutzer-Str. 12
76684 Oestringen
Germany
Proofreading/ Editing: Oliver Nova
Cover: Kim Nusko
Translation: DeepL
ISBN: 9798686468740
Proofreading EN: Walter Streetberg

Email: Benjamin-Spahic@web.de
Facebook: Benjamin Spahic
3D printing engineering without prior knowledge
First publication 15.09.2020
Distribution through kindledirectpublishing
Amazon Media EU S.à r.l., 5 Rue Plaetis, L-2338, Luxembourg

Disclaimer

Printed in Great Britain
by Amazon

38349583R00066